ENGLISH GARDENS

JOHN CURTIS

Text by Richard Ashby

SALMON

INTRODUCTION

It is surely true that there is something spiritual about making a garden and tending it. It is no accident that in the Bible the earliest encounter man has with God is in the Garden of Eden and in the near east, where that garden is set, the ancient word for garden translates as 'paradise'. Alongside their spiritual significance go earthly pleasures. Gardens are a place for illicit trysts, the meeting place of lovers, a solace in old age and a place for games and merriment. They are a delight for all the five senses. They are a place for relaxation and pleasure, an opportunity to leave the cares of the world and indeed to rest from the labour of making the garden itself. For gardening is both enjoyable and hard work.

The English have a special affinity with gardening and wherever the English go they make gardens. But English gardening has been a victim of changing fashions and what was appropriate in one century was decidedly not in the next. Gardens continue to evolve drawing inspiration from home and abroad. This book has examples of a whole range of English gardens, almost all of which might be regarded as 'typical' and yet often very different to each other. That is the glory of creating a garden; it can be what ever its owner wants it to be and a reflection of their beliefs. Each is a creation of a bit of heaven on earth. From the humblest front garden to the great sweeping Arcadian landscapes, the English garden is a foretaste of paradise.

Levens Hall, *Cumbria*

CHATSWORTH HOUSE, *Derbyshire*

Chatsworth is garden history made real. It was worked on by some of the greatest names in English gardens and it reflects the changing fashions of three centuries with its sweeping lawns, lakes, fountains and cascades, grand landscaping and serpentine paths, statues and grottos, conservatories, formal flower-beds and informal dells.

WESTBURY COURT, *Gloucestershire*

This 17th century Dutch water garden is a rare survivor of a style which was largely swept away in the passion for informal landscaping which came a century later. The long straight canals, the neatly clipped hedges, flowering bulbs, fruit trees and evergreens make for a formal garden centred on a gazebo from which it can all be viewed.

ASHTON-UNDER-HILL, *Worcestershire*

Although the main concern of the country dweller was to put food on the table, flowers would often be planted along the paths or bordering the vegetable beds. It was largely those with a little leisure who made up village 'society', the doctor, the vicar, retired professional people, ladies of independent means and with time on their hands, who developed the cottage garden into what we know today. Their efforts were enhanced by the popular painters of the middle to late 19th century who created a rural idyll with their images of happy families in their cottage gardens. The image has become reality and the country cottage, with its garden a profusion of colours, is an aspiration of us all.

SAPPERTON, *Gloucestershire*

The clipping of box and yew and other small leafed trees into fantastic shapes goes back at least to Roman times and was very fashionable in 17th century formal gardens. The 18th century landscaping movements swept most of it away, but an entire topiary garden survives at Levens Hall in Cumbria, while here at Sapperton a whimsical house mirroring the cottage behind is a more recent and modest example of the art.

WREST PARK, *Bedfordshire*
'Parterres' were introduced into England from France where they had been a favourite of Henrietta Maria, the French wife of Charles I. They became very popular with their neatly cut box hedging, their gravel or sanded paths and their neat scythed grass.

LYME PARK, *Cheshire*
The Victorians loved colour in their gardens. With the revival of formal gardening and wit it the idea of 'controlling nature' again, the parterre had a new lease of life, now with a riot of colour but framed still by the formal box hedge and the gravel path.

BURY ST EDMUNDS, *Suffolk*

The formal gardening which the Victorians so enjoyed found something of a climax in the establishment of municipal parks for which Joseph Paxton, who had been head gardener at Chatsworth and who designed the Crystal Palace for the Great Exhibition in 1851, gained a reputation as a designer. The movement tried to ameliorate the dreadful conditions of the poor by providing them with space, light and air where they could enjoy themselves amidst beautiful gardens. The geometric patterns and carpet bedding were decried by some for their garish colours and lack of subtlety, but in a sense they reflect the purpose of the park itself, which was to direct the energies and pleasures of the poor aright. The park also had a moral purpose: no swearing, no gambling, no drink!

BATH, *Somerset*

In the private parks of the city of Bath there would certainly be no drunkenness or bad behaviour for the poor were kept out by admission charges in that select city. Today, however, they are open to all and everyone can enjoy the gardens for which the city and its council are justly famed. Bath is a regular winner of the 'Britain in Bloom' Competition.

NEAR WESTONBIRT, *Gloucestershire*

The blend of Cotswold architecture, Cotswold stone and cottage gardens is deeply satisfying. It is no wonder that the area attracted men like William Morris and craftsmen influenced by him. The cottages and their surrounding gardens were taken as the ideal pattern of good domestic living and were greatly influential in the Arts and Crafts movement at the end of the 19th century and for much longer in the 'garden cities'.

CASTLE ACRE PRIORY, *Norfolk*

In many religious traditions people have felt the need to live away from the world in order to pursue the spiritual life. The monastery was, as far as possible, a self-contained community largely dependent on its own resources. Its farms contained sheep, cattle, pigs and hens while the stew-ponds provided fish for meatless Fridays and the fast of Lent. A medieval plan of an idealised monastery shows eighteen beds for vegetables, mostly root crops. Alongside these staples of daily life was the herb garden, important in an age before modern medicine, when medicinal herbs were used to treat the ailments of the inhabitants. The regular contacts between the religious houses of Europe brought many new herbs to England, and the current garden is planted with herbs that would have been familiar in medieval times.

THORNBURY, *Gloucestershire*

Plots of land were often provided for the workers in the new industrial towns both for growing vegetables for their own tables and also to encourage self-sufficiency (not a new idea) and sober living. By the 19th century they were often provided by the new municipal councils and gardening clubs and vegetable competitions flourished. Allotments became of great importance in the two world wars when the 'dig for victory' movement enabled the country to feed itself again. Parks were dug up and every available space was used to grow food to relieve the rather spartan wartime-rationed diet. With peacetime and the rise of the supermarket and packaged food, many allotments fell into disuse, but there has been a great revival as people have become more interested in what they eat, and how it is grown.

HUTTON LE HOLE, *North Yorkshire*

Mankind has grown vegetables since earliest times. The broad bean was being cultivated in the Iron Age and growing vegetables and salad crops for the kitchen was part of the work in the monasteries. The great houses had their own kitchen gardens and country people always grew much of their own food. Vegetables were the priority in the traditional cottage garden but many had flowers too, often grown side by side and in perfect harmony.

HIDCOTE MANOR, *Gloucestershire*

The wonderful Arts and Crafts garden at
Hidcote was begun by an American, Lawrence
Johnston. A number of different gardens have
been created in 'outdoor rooms', each with
a different name and theme and separated by
tall hedges. Influenced by such luminaries as
the architect Sir Edward Lutyens and gardener
Gertrude Jekyll, Hidcote is, nevertheless
unique and in a class of its own.

PACKWOOD HOUSE, *Warwickshire*

There can be something deeply spiritual
about a garden and gardening. Perhaps it
is the sense of being at one with nature,
even if it is 'nature tamed'. Perhaps it is
working with living things, watching
plants grow and developing the patience
which is a necessary virtue while nature
does her part of the work. Individual
plants have meanings or connections with
religious events or holy people and
sometimes the garden itself has an explicit
religious meaning or symbolism. The Yew
Garden at Packwood, begun by a Puritan
lawyer and believed to date from the 17th
century, is interpreted as a representation
of Christ's 'Sermon on the Mount'.
A mount is topped by a great yew known
as 'The Master'. Nearby are the 'twelve
apostles' and then the multitude, which
is a later planting and frames a delightful
vista of the manor house.

ALNWICK CASTLE, *Northumberland*
Under the direction of the Duchess of
Northumberland, two renowned Belgian
garden designers have created a garden for
the new millennium. It includes a woodland
walk, a labyrinth, a poison garden and a great
tree house. At its centre is a grand cascade
down which more than 7,000 gallons of
water a minute tumble over 21 steps.

STAINDROP, *County Durham*
While the great lords had their statuary and
their classical temples, what did the ordinary
man have? The garden gnome arrived from
Germany around 1847 and, along with
plaster toadstools, animals and birds, has
been firmly part of domestic gardening ever
since. This little front garden is a riot of
colourful plants and ornaments.

PAINSWICK ROCOCO GARDEN, *Gloucestershire*

Rococo is an architectural term which has only recently been applied to 18th century gardens characterised by irregular and whimsical design and an eclectic mix of building styles. Painswick garden was largely lost by the 1970s but has since been wonderfully restored. The snowdrops in spring are quite spectacular.

MELFORD HALL, *Suffolk*

Our forefathers often preferred to view their gardens from above. The little back gardens of Georgian town houses were designed to be viewed from its windows. In larger gardens a special viewing house would be built which would also be used for refreshments. This Jacobean-style example stands in the garden of the Elizabethan Melford Hall.

BLENHEIM PALACE, *Oxfordshire*

The landscaped park at Blenheim is one of the finest achievements of the age of the great landscape gardeners. Nearer the house, the great water terraces are the product of the 20th century, though they hark back to the formal Italianate gardens which were popular before the landscaping revolution. Blenheim shows that the two can live in harmony and enhance each other.

ANGLESEY ABBEY, *Cambridgeshire*

It was not until 1930 that the owner, Lord Fairhaven, began to create a great garden in the flat lands of the Fens where there had once been an Augustinian priory. Its gardens within a garden give year-long colour and interest and its collection of classical statuary is very fine.

BELSAY HALL, *Northumberland*

As the landscape movement developed so the 'picturesque' became increasingly important and the owners of the great houses started to look for ways of introducing dramatic elements into their gardens. At Belsay a quarry was incorporated into the garden providing an impressive contrast to the more pastoral delights of the earlier landscaped park.

TATTON PARK, *Cheshire*

When Japan became accessible to the West from 1868 there was immediately a great interest in Japanese art and culture and especially gardens. Demand for acers and flowering cherries rocketed. At Tatton the garden was created by Japanese gardeners using only plants of Japanese origin and includes a temple, a pagoda and simple bridges. The cranes add a nice touch.

DUNGENESS, *Kent*

Gardeners have to contend with both the vagaries of the English climate and a great variety of soil conditions. Nowhere are the conditions as difficult as by the sea where strong, salt laden, winds are detrimental to tender plants. In one of the most difficult situations the film director, Derek Jarman, set about transforming the barren shingle into an exotic, unique garden, using carefully chosen plants which would be hardy in the inhospitable terrain and decorating it with driftwood and flotsam picked up on his beach-combing trips along the sea-shore. The garden is a testament to one man's struggle both against the elements and the illness from which he was to die and in a strange parallel is both threatened by and yet defies the great nuclear power station nearby.

ALNWICK, *Northumberland*

Municipal gardeners often prided themselves on the elaborate designs which could be achieved and railway engines, cartoon characters animals or buildings would be replicated, often in three dimensions. The floral clock has become something of a seaside town cliché, but this modest version in a small country town is charming.

SHEFFIELD PARK, *East Sussex*
This garden was laid out by the great 'Capability' Brown. What we see today, though, is largely the work of the 20th century where the landscaping of the 18th century is brought together with planting of a wide range of trees and shrubs to create a garden which is full of colour. The rhododendrons are spectacular.

STOURHEAD, *Wiltshire*
Stourhead is perhaps the best of the English landscape gardens, an art which England gave to the world. It is a re-creation of the Arcadian landscapes of the Latin writer Virgil and of the 17th century painter Poussin in an English valley. A walk round the lake is an ever-changing experience of enclosed scene and dramatic vista. The banks of the lake are enlivened with temples, a grotto with a reclining nymph and a river god's cave, and a Gothic cottage. Nearby is the old Bristol High Cross and on the higher ground a pantheon, a temple to all the gods, and further away, King Alfred's Tower is outside the main circuit. The little village of Stourton with its parish church and inn are incorporated into the idyllic scene.

NEW COLLEGE, OXFORD

By the end of the 19th century the passion that the Victorians had for controlling nature and for garish bedding was over, to be replaced with something more subtle and natural. The Arts and Crafts movement showed the way away from mass production to pride in craftsmanship and the same thing happened in gardening. Out went formal design and carpet bedding and in came herbaceous borders and natural materials. Two women were influential more than any others for this evolution. Gertrude Jekyll knew William Morris and her books set out the principles for her followers. Between the two world wars Vita Sackville-West created Sissinghurst, like Hidcote, based on garden rooms of contrasting styles. At New College the medieval wall shelters the herbaceous border; a garden for learned contemplation!

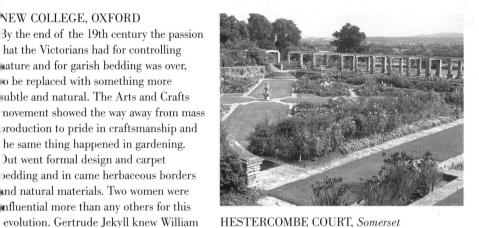

HESTERCOMBE COURT, *Somerset*

Good architecture and gardening go together. Gertrude Jekyll was a friend of the architect Edwin Lutyens and they often worked together. Her gardens and his houses complemented each other. At Hestercombe they collaborated on the garden design where her informality and the richness of the planting perfectly complement the formality of the plan.

CHRIST'S PIECES, CAMBRIDGE

Christ's Pieces was acquired by the City of Cambridge from Jesus College in 1884 to be a public garden in the centre of the busy city. As well as flower gardens there are bowling greens and tennis courts and over 10,000 daffodil bulbs make a spectacular show in the spring. Although surrounded by busy roads this oasis is much appreciated by the people of Cambridge who have steadfastly refused to sacrifice any of it for the expansion of a nearby bus station.

Published in Great Britain by J. Salmon Ltd., Sevenoaks, Kent TN13 1BB. Telephone 01732 452381. Email enquiries@jsalmon.co.uk.
Design by John Curtis. Text and photographs © John Curtis. All rights reserved. No part of this book may be produced, stored in a retrieval system or transmitted in any form or by any means without prior written permission of the publishers.
ISBN 1-84640-033-3   Printed in Slovenia © 2006 Photograph on page 22 by kind permission of His Grace, the Duke of Marlborough.

Title page photograph: Hestercombe, *Somerset*
Front cover photograph: Sissinghurst Castle, *Kent*.   Back cover photograph: Botanic Gardens, *Oxford*